Camp Panda

Helping Cubs Return to the Wild

For the wild bunch of neighborhood kids (who are no longer kids):
Sydney, Colton, Kyle, Victoria, Jameson, Simon, and Jaimie.

Catherine Thimmesh
SIBERT MEDALIST

Camp Panda

Helping Cubs Return to the Wild

Houghton Mifflin Harcourt

Boston | New York

Prologue

Lumbering down the grassy mountainside in southwestern China—being careful not to slip—is a giant panda teddy bear. It is black and white and fluffy and fuzzy, and it walks upright, unassisted—which is odd for a teddy bear of any species or size. Odder still is the fact that its teddy bear arms are wrapped tightly around a roly-poly furball who squirms and makes noises—announcing to the world that he isn't stuffed with fluff. He's a living, breathing baby panda cub.

Pandas In Peril

Deep in the forest, high in the mountains—amidst the evergreens, the firs, the spruces—sits a giant panda. She's plopped herself on the forest floor, and she munches bamboo shoot after bamboo shoot. It's hard for humans to cut through bamboo with an ax, but the panda peels and eats a single bamboo shoot in forty seconds! She chomps on bamboo sixteen hours a day, every day. Except . . . when she doesn't.

There are typically only two reasons why a female panda would stop the bamboo eat-a-thon: if she were giving birth or tending to her new cub. A newborn panda cub is exceptionally fragile: weighing only four ounces, blind, hairless, unable to walk (or crawl or scoot), unable to feed itself, and, somewhat surprisingly, unable to poop by itself (which can prove deadly). So for several days Mama Panda will not leave her cub's side even for a moment.

RIGHT: A giant panda in the Wolong Nature Reserve in Sichuan Province, China. The iconic round face of the panda is not chubbiness; it's due to massive cheek muscles. The cheek and jaw muscles are so powerful, they easily bite through the thickest bamboo stalks.

A mama panda with her eighteen-day-old cub at Chimelong Safari Park in Guangzhou. While it appears that they are looking at each other, the cub cannot see until it is forty days old. By one month old, the distinctive black-and-white markings that are starting to appear will be fully developed.

Eventually, though, she secures her newborn in the den and heads back to the bamboo thicket to feast—crucial for her own survival as well as her cub's. Resting on the forest floor, surrounded by her main food source, and munching contentedly, she is completely unaware of the precarious situation she is in—that her whole species is in.

She is unaware of just how few pandas are left in the world, unaware that the giant panda—so rare and beautiful and beloved—is vulnerable. Vulnerable, and at risk of becoming extinct in the wild.

PICKY EATER

Pandas have evolved to eat a very special diet—almost exclusively bamboo. Because of bamboo's low nutrient value, a panda must eat between twenty and forty pounds a day, even in winter, to gain the nutrition it needs. (This explains why the panda bear doesn't hibernate.)

The problem with this diet (aside from being difficult to digest) is that bamboo plants have periodic massive flowering periods—followed by massive die-offs. When these die-offs occur, the pandas' source of food in an area completely and instantly disappears—putting the pandas in grave danger if they cannot locate more bamboo within their habitat.

A giant panda in the Wolong Nature Reserve chomps on bamboo. There are roughly twenty-five varieties of bamboo plants grown in the area where the pandas currently live. Pandas particularly like the umbrella, arrow, and golden bamboo varieties.

Then & Now

P andas are in peril *because* of humans! We caused the problem, so we have a responsibility to help fix it," exclaims Suzanne Braden, who, after visiting China and the Wolong Nature Reserve, was so moved by the plight of the panda that, when she returned to the United States, she cofounded the nonprofit Pandas International to help save the magnificent species.

Roughly a thousand years ago, an estimated twenty-three thousand pandas roamed wild and free through many thousands of miles of pristine, tranquil habitat in their native China—cool, moist forests of mixed broadleaf trees, with plenty of canopy coverage and an abundance of bamboo. But within the last forty years, more than 50 percent of the panda's already shrinking habitat has been destroyed by humans—sliced and diced and reduced to six small pockets of isolated land areas, most in southern China. This was a direct result of the growth of agriculture and industrialization, and an unprecedented growth—more of an explosion, actually—in the human population.

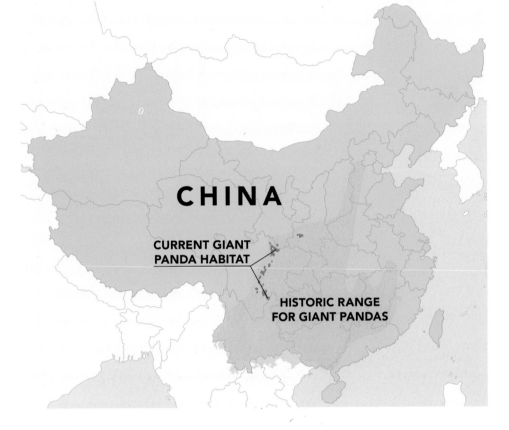

CHINA

CURRENT GIANT PANDA HABITAT

HISTORIC RANGE FOR GIANT PANDAS

The number of Chinese people grew from five hundred million in the 1950s to one billion just thirty years later and roughly 1.4 billion people today. (In comparison, the United States has about 325 million people.) More and more people meant more and more land needed for homes, businesses, schools, and farms. More agriculture meant more and more land was needed for planting crops and raising livestock. And infrastructure projects meant using more and more land to build roads, railways, bridges, and dams.

Much of this land was territory the panda traditionally roamed. Huge swaths of forest were logged and cleared out, obliterating vast areas and rendering them unsuitable for panda habitat.

It must have been a terrifying time for the pandas: *chop chop chop, whoo whoo!, beep beep*—a cacophony of noise and chaos encroaching on their homes, destroying their food, their shelter . . . sending them scampering away to unfamiliar lands, higher and higher in the mountains.

A panda at Wolong hides out by a tree. For pandas here, as well as those in other reserves and in captivity, keepers are often able to distinguish one animal from another by the shape and size of their black eye patches; they all vary slightly.

Not only were pandas put at risk primarily due to habitat destruction and habitat encroachment by humans, but they were also shot and killed by humans: by trophy hunters (before hunting pandas was banned), by poachers (illegally killing pandas anyway, usually for their fur), and by local villagers protecting their livestock.

It was estimated that by the 1980s, a mere one thousand pandas remained in the wild. By 1990, they were officially declared an endangered species.

Pandas are beloved the world over, but nowhere more so than in their home country, where they are considered a national treasure. The *ooh*ing and *aah*ing people express toward the inky-eyed panda have made the bear not only an international sensation— but the de facto symbol of China itself. It appears that the Chinese government is thoroughly committed to protecting its black-and-white crown jewel.

So far, Suzanne Braden reports, poaching has been nearly eliminated—thanks to extreme penalties that can include up to ten years behind bars. Sixty-seven nature reserves have been designated as protected panda habitats (although habitat fragmentation—the segmenting of one large area into smaller, isolated pockets—remains a huge problem). Reforestation and bamboo planting efforts are ongoing, as is local community outreach and education. And a robust captive breeding program in China helps ensure a growing panda population.

In the Wolong Nature Reserve, Cao Cao and her cub Tao Tao enjoy some together time. Over the years, the Chinese language has given the giant panda more than twenty different names, including spotted bear, bamboo bear, giant bear cat, and bear cat. The scientific name for the giant panda is *Ailuropoda melanoleuca*.

And now, to further the panda conservation efforts, the China Conservation and Research Center for the Giant Panda (CCRCGP) is working on a comprehensive three-stage program to reintroduce pandas into the wild—a program that often involves scientists dressed as giant panda teddy bears. It's a boot camp of sorts — Camp Panda — wilderness training for panda cubs.

The ultimate goal of any reintroduction program is to create a *self-sustaining* population in the wild—a species that can survive and breed completely on its own, with no human intervention. Critical in this survival equation is genetic diversity (the variation in the amount of genetic information within a species). It is the key to species adaptability and to healthy populations—providing the greatest chance for species survival when faced with external, environmental changes.

"There has been an exponential growth in reintroductions because the science and management actions have matured so much that they are frequently successful," explains Dr. Axel Moehrenschlager, the chair of IUCN's (International Union for Conservation of Nature) Reintroduction Specialist Group and the director of conservation and science at the Calgary Zoo in Alberta, Canada. "And secondly," Axel continues, "in many situations, the level of desperation keeps increasing. Often, if other conservation techniques are not able to prevent extinction on their own, reintroductions are necessary to help save a species."*

In some reintroduction efforts, the animals actually have to be trained—taught—how to be wild: how to find food, avoid predators, seek shelter. Pandas are one such species. Baby panda cubs are not born with an innate set of survival skills. These skills must be taught (and learned!) before a cub is released or the cub will have no chance in the wild.

"The tricky thing with reintroductions is that they are not guaranteed to work," says Axel. "But most of the time, the alternative of doing nothing means extinction."*

In order to minimize direct contact, when scientists and researchers need to transport a cub in the reintroduction program they first put on full panda costumes and then put the cub in a basket, a plastic bin, or a cage.

Reality Check

G one are the dinosaurs. Gone, the woolly mammoths, the saber-toothed tigers. They vanished a long, long time ago. But even today—right here, right now—thousands of species, such as the panda, are vulnerable and endangered. Whole species are disappearing from our planet at a terrifying pace—a thousand times the natural rate (which is defined as the loss of one to five species per year). Twenty-two *thousand* species are currently at risk of extinction. Surely there are thousands more on the brink—as yet to be identified.

"I tend to be very conservative in these kinds of statements because I hate fearmongering," says Dr. Axel Moehrenschlager. *"But, unfortunately, the reality is that every day when we wake up, we've probably lost another three species on the planet."*

That's more than a thousand species . . . every year.

Most alarmingly, these statistics indicate that we are currently in the midst of a sixth *mass extinction*—a mass dying-off of species. From amphibians and reptiles to birds and mammals, no biological class is immune. Recently lost species include the golden toad, the po'ouli (a Hawaiian bird), the West African black rhino, the Tecopa pupfish, the Pyrenean ibex, the Zanzibar leopard, the Round Island burrowing boa, and the Pinta Island tortoise—to name just a few. There have been five mass species extinctions in Earth's past—the most well known, of course, being that of the dinosaurs.

"But, unlike any of the other mass extinctions," explains Axel, "this one is quite clearly being caused by just one species—humans. And so it has a disproportionate and powerful effect: one species affecting the millions of others."

Species are dying off in unprecedented numbers because of poaching and overhunting; because of habitat destruction and habitat encroachment; because of pollution and poisons in the air, ground, and water; and because of the abnormal effects of global climate change.

In 2000, there were only ten remaining West African black rhinos in the world, all in Cameroon, zero in captivity. The next year, only five remained. By 2006, not one had been spotted—nor was there any evidence of their existence. By 2011, the West African black rhino was officially declared extinct, thanks to poachers who mercilessly killed them for their horns—which people then use for decorative carvings and grind into powder for medicines. The West African black rhinoceros was a subspecies of the critically endangered black rhino (the rhino shown in this photo).

But every day, conservation scientists and experts and volunteers around the globe desperately work to save thousands of vulnerable and endangered species. They use a variety of methods, often simultaneously: protection of habitat, replanting of habitat, stricter laws to prevent poaching, community awareness—and reintroducing animals back into the wild.

"If you've found a species that's almost gone to extinction," says Axel, "then something's gone terribly wrong . . . and you have to overwhelm that negative influence through action and science and learning."

With the panda, all of these conservation efforts have been employed, with reintroductions being the most recent—and perhaps the most ambitious—effort yet.

The reality of the current mass extinction—and the sheer volume of animals close to or on the brink—is cause for great alarm.

But every ongoing attempt at saving a species means two things: the species is not yet gone . . . and . . . there is still hope.

These species would most likely be extinct were it not for human intervention. They have undergone or are currently involved in successful reintroductions to the wild: Karner blue butterfly, red wolf, black-footed ferret, whooping crane, golden-lion tamarin.

What Hope Looks Like

T he panda reintroduction program began in 2003 with a team made up of researchers from many fields, including ecology, behavioral science, veterinary, and feeding management," explains Suzanne Braden of Pandas International.

The ambitious reintroduction program began in the Wolong Nature Reserve in China's Sichuan Province, spearheaded by the Chinese Conservation and Research Center for the Giant Panda (CCRCGP) under the leadership of Zhang Hemin—affectionately known as Papa Panda. After much research, study, testing, and consulting, the team chose the first panda for freedom in the wild: Xiang Xiang, a captive-born and -raised cub who was roughly two years old when training began. He was chosen for his good health and his apparent strength and skills.

It is hard to take a captive panda—one that's been dependent on humans its whole life—erase that dependency, and replace it with an unfamiliar self-sufficiency.

Xiang Xiang takes a break from eating bamboo to hang out in his training enclosure. The giant panda has a special, thick lining in its throat to protect against bamboo splinters. Its stomach is similarly protected. Adult pandas like Xiang Xiang weigh anywhere from about 200 pounds to 350 pounds. They grow to a length of roughly four to six feet (from the bottom of the hind feet to the top of the head).

But the plight of the world's most beloved bear demanded that Zhang Hemin and the team at CCRCGP try.

To begin training, Huang Yan, the deputy chief engineer and head of the wilderness training program for CCRCGP, moved Xiang Xiang from his captive environment (where he regularly interacted with people and pandas) to a larger, semi-wild enclosure where the team attempted to prepare him for his new life in the wild. The scientists relied on active research and the best scientifically based assumptions they could make. Still, Zhang Hemin and Huang Yan recognized that this first attempt would also be mostly trial and error.

As the training progressed, the team of scientists gradually reduced their contact with Xiang Xiang so he could learn to interact with the wild environment on his own.

A member of the reintroduction team checks in on Xiang Xiang in his training enclosure.

ABOVE: Zhang Hemin, Papa Panda (center, holding instrument, looking at monitor), along with team members at CCRCGP, performs a medical procedure on one of the pandas. Zhang Hemin has been working with pandas for over thirty years. He spends all year out in the field, taking care of the pandas and managing CCRCGP's programs.

LEFT: Huang Yan, head of the reintroduction program at CCRCGP, discusses his work while in the monitoring room. The bank of video screens in the background provides constant surveillance on the pandas in the training enclosures, making it easier to monitor and learn about panda behavior, as well as keep an eye out for danger.

...ng Xiang's diet had been subsidized with manufactured foods

...foods were gradually withdrawn and replaced solely with his new,
...nboo, bamboo, bamboo. In the first few weeks, alas, poor Xiang Xiang
...d panda technique of bamboo eating—he wasted about 75 percent of
...robably spent much of those days hungry.

But a... ...in 2006, Huang Yan and the team declared Xiang Xiang ready for release. The panda r... ...to be lured into the transport cage, so a tranquilizer dart was used. Once asleep, he was given a final medical checkup, fitted with a radio tracking collar, and, after a night in the hospital, transported to the release site. With plenty of dignitaries present and fanfare fit for a king, the release cage was opened. Xiang Xiang wandered out, looked around for a moment—bemused? confused?—and then scampered off into the woods.

Xiang Xiang is released into the wild. Although pandas are typically thought of as cuddly and harmless, they have enormously powerful jaws and claws and can be quite dangerous—hence the officer in riot gear making sure Xiang Xiang doesn't walk into the crowd.

Two CCRCGP team members use radio telemetry equipment to track one of the released pandas. The panda's radio collar beams a signal that the tracking equipment can hone in on to provide the animal's location coordinates.

Huang Yan and the team members tracked and monitored Xiang Xiang, and they could tell that he started out successfully: building a den, foraging for food. But sadly, a year later, the trial ended suddenly when he was found dead.

"Xiang Xiang, the first panda released, was critically injured and didn't survive," recalls Suzanne. *"So the program was put on hold for several years while they studied the flaws and redesigned their approach based on what they had learned."*

Zhang Hemin, Huang Yan, and the experts on the CCRCGP team concluded that the five-year-old Xiang Xiang lacked sufficient survival skills. He was released in an area "heavily" populated with wild pandas, and they think he probably fought with other males over females and mating, eventually leading him to seek shelter in a tree—which he fell out of, causing his death.

With reintroductions, often the situation for a species is so dire—and the threat of extinction so imminent—that it's necessary for conservationists to jump in and try

something before it's too late. Sometimes this means that research goes hand in hand with the implementation of the program—they gather data and learn as they go along.

One year, Huang Yan and his team hosted a scientific forum to discuss their panda reintroduction efforts with experts around the world who were involved in other species reintroduction programs. Presentations were given on the Mexican wolf, the black rhino, the red wolf, the black-footed ferret, the snub-nosed monkey, and others. The sharing of scientific milestones and setbacks was beneficial to all involved, because even though the species differed—and what might work with a wolf, for example, might not succeed with a snub-nosed monkey—some of the techniques and overall approaches could be applicable across species, or even modified to fit a given species.

The CCRCGP team learned that many reintroduction efforts must shift strategy midway through—and this isn't a bad thing; on the contrary, it's how the best scientists work. If the data does not support the original hypothesis and experimentation (or implementation), then the original hypothesis and approach must be changed.

And so Zhang Hemin, Huang Yan, and the rest of the team did indeed change their approach.

Cao Cao and her cub Tao Tao are the first pandas to undergo reintroduction training under the new approach. It will be several years before data will be available to support or reject the new methods.

Change Comes

One of the key elements that the experts agreed on for their new approach was to eliminate any human contact with the panda cubs in training. Thus, in time, serious scientists would be playing make-believe—disguising themselves in fuzzy-furry giant panda costumes.

That might prove good for the pandas, but the team members weren't particularly comfortable in the heavy, hot panda suits. It was hard to see things clearly, and their range of motion was severely hampered by the cumbersome costumes. And they stink! Panda poo and pee are rubbed all over their "fur" so that they'll smell like a panda and not a person.

Still, the cub isn't fooled. Not entirely. The giant teddy bear might look—and sort of smell—like his mama, but the touch and the taste and the sounds (pandas are known to make thirteen distinct sounds!) and so many other little things are clearly different.

Researchers, dressed in their panda suits, have a sit-down with Tao Tao and give him a general medical checkup: measuring his growth, looking for injuries, etc. Like a curious small child, Tao Tao appears interested in the blue notebook—or maybe he's just squirming to get away!

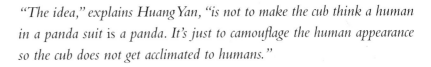

"The idea," explains Huang Yan, *"is not to make the cub think a human in a panda suit* is *a panda. It's just to camouflage the human appearance so the cub does not get acclimated to humans."*

For a panda to survive in the wild, a panda must *be* wild—and that can't happen if it's been cuddled and coddled and cared for by humans before it's released. Yet it will take two years of "wilderness training" in the newly developed reintroduction program before a panda cub is set free, and some human interaction is unavoidable. Thus, the costumes.

But the costuming was only step one of several other strategic changes that Zhang Hemin and Huang Yan's team would make. Step two: put the mama panda back in charge (just as she would be in the wild).

PANDAS ONLY

It's crucial that pandas in the release program not become acclimated to humans, for several reasons. First, it trains the cubs not to depend on humans providing for them.

Instead, it encourages and reinforces the cubs' natural behaviors in seeking out their own food, water, and shelter. Second, it encourages a healthy fear of humans—discouraging the cubs from wandering onto farms and being shot by farmers protecting their livelihoods.

Fear of humans also sends the pandas scurrying for cover should people approach them—critical for avoiding poachers who are (illegally) out to kill them.

Tao Tao submits to a checkup.

27

Some of the CCRCGP team members (along with two journalists in center). From left to right, the team members are: Qiu Yu, Mu Shi Jie, Dong Chao, Deng Lin Hua (the head vet), and Huang Yan.

No longer would non-pandas (i.e., humans) try to teach a panda how to actually *be a* panda. Step three, another significant realization, concerned the timing of the release.

"It was determined that a cub should be released when it's about two years of age," says Suzanne Braden, of Pandas International. "That is the natural timing when a mother would push a cub away to find its own territory, so it's a more natural separation."

During this period of redesign, researchers faced an additional and even bigger setback. In 2008, a horrific, devastating earthquake in Sichuan, China, left tens of thousands of people dead, millions homeless, thousands of buildings destroyed, and untold damage to natural lands and habitats—an epic disaster that also left behind the destruction of the Wolong Panda Research Center. Unsurprisingly, the reintroduction program was put on hold. The pandas would have to wait to be returned to the wild.

REINTRODUCTION

Of all the reintroductions of all the different species that are undertaken, only a small percentage currently have elaborate training-to-be-wild programs. For many species—because of their biology, because of their behavior—there's just not a whole lot you can do other than simply release them into the wild (known as a "hard" release) and then hope for the best.

But there are many reintroduction efforts that don't do hard releases yet do employ some type of acclimation process, where the species is slowly transitioned back into the wild—using a staged, or "soft," release.

The giant panda is in fact part of the bear family (not the raccoon family as many had argued for years). Its closest relative is the spectacled bear of South America.

Habitat Critical

Meanwhile, other endeavors to save the panda continued—particularly those attempting to ensure a healthy, diverse habitat for them. And because of these ongoing efforts, huge ecological side benefits have been attained and continue to be achieved. That's because the panda is known as an "umbrella species." By protecting the panda—and, by necessary extension, its habitat—conservationists are also indirectly protecting the many other species that share the panda's ecosystem, that are under its "umbrella."

"If you can conserve the space that the pandas need," explains Colby Loucks of the World Wildlife Fund (WWF), "you're saving one of the more diverse, temperate forests and subtropical rainforests in the world. . . . As an umbrella species, the panda also encounters all the mountainous species living there, including red pandas, pheasants, golden snub-nosed monkeys, takins, snow leopards, deer, and lots of bird species."

Three species under the panda umbrella: the snow leopard, the golden snub-nosed monkey, the red panda.

The golden snub-nosed monkey, for example, is categorized as an endangered animal, but it has received very little in terms of attention or conservation dollars. Because 96 percent of the pandas' habitat overlaps with areas where many animals (such as the golden snub-nosed monkey) exist exclusively, if that habitat is saved, the monkeys can be saved, too.

The umbrella also helps humans, by protecting that ecosystem. For example, roughly one hundred million people live in adjacent areas, and six hundred million people live downstream from the pandas' mountainous habitat. They all depend upon clean, unpolluted water channeled from the rainwater running through that territory into the rivers and streams.

Every effort comes with challenges. At times, policies intended to preserve habitats have in turn hurt the local villagers. And in an ironic twist, the adoration of pandas has led to ecotourism—which is a boon to the local economy and the villagers, but has unwittingly destroyed some panda habitats (one example: horses brought in to transport tourists trampled and ate large areas of bamboo!). Understanding the interconnectedness between humans and natural ecosystems is a key element in the quest for panda sustainability.

"We have been focusing on identifying how a panda habitat changes over time and across space," says Jianguo "Jack" Liu of Michigan State University's Center for Systems Integration and Sustainability, one of the many independent institutions working alongside the CCRCGP. "This is very important because when you release pandas, you need to know where the good places to release pandas are. We need to release pandas in good habitat so that they can survive and sustain themselves for a long time. We also need to understand how climate change might affect their habitat, so we can be sure pandas new to the wild will be secure there for many years."

An old-growth, or primary, forest habitat of the panda in southern China. Even though pandas get most of the water they need from bamboo, they still need water from streams or rivers for survival.

Not only do scientists need to find ways to protect panda habitats—and grow them through reforestation and bamboo planting—they also need to reconnect the fragmented areas wherever possible.

Good, healthy habitats are critical for any species' survival. Unfortunately, probably the greatest current threat to giant pandas—and to their reintroduction success—is the severe fragmentation of their habitat. Land has been cut by roads, railways, and dams into smaller, isolated spaces. If the pandas are too isolated, they might be unable to find a mate or a source of food.

"Ultimately, at the end of the day," explains Colby Loucks, "you need habitat and protection for pandas. You can reintroduce a thousand of them—but unless they have some space to live, it won't work in the long term."

One way to connect these fragmented areas is by building "green corridors" (strips of land that connect fragments of habitat to each other) so the animals can move within and between their habitat to find food (especially important if there is a mass bamboo die-off) and find mates (especially important because pandas must reproduce in the wild to sustain the population, hopefully diversifying the gene pool along the way).

PANDAS OR PEOPLE

Pandas need many trees and vast forest cover in their habitat . . . for survival. Villagers need to chop down trees to build fires to cook with and to heat their homes . . . for survival.

Jack Liu's research helped inform a government intervention with the five thousand villagers living in the reserve areas in an attempt to find a win-win solution to this problem. The government provided monetary subsidies to the villagers to pay their electric bills so that they would use electricity for heating and cooking rather than chopping down trees and burning wood. The tradeoff was that the villagers would no longer have a reason to cut down trees from the pandas' habitat. In the initial six years following this policy change, the forest cover increased by 5 percent—a marked improvement for the habitat and thus for panda survival that hopefully will only increase.

A secondary forest panda habitat. The trees are not as dense as in a primary forest because this forest has been logged. This alteration from its natural state is what makes it a secondary forest. Pandas play a crucial role in these forests by spreading seeds while they roam about—helping regrow forest plants.

Critically for the giant panda—and all the species under its umbrella—the government and the conservationists are collaborating, attacking the many pieces of the habitat puzzle.

"I believe that investing in and conserving the habitat, limiting the amount of fragmentation, working with communities so they can also conserve the panda habitat around them, will accomplish the critical things to ensure that pandas are around in the future," says WWF's Colby Loucks. "I don't think the Chinese government would ever want to let giant pandas go extinct," he adds. "Their panda conservation efforts have been so successful that the giant panda has become an international symbol for conserving wildlife."

Dissent

But there are those who disagree. They do not necessarily *want* the panda to go extinct, but they feel that nature should just take its course, and whatever happens, happens.

Critics point out that the species is ill-suited for long-term survival. Exhibit one: their bamboo-only diet is too restrictive—limiting their habitat and potentially starving them with massive bamboo die-offs. Exhibit two: their breeding is ridiculously difficult, given the narrow time frame—just two to seven days a year when the female is in heat and receptive to mating. And within that time frame, there are just twenty-four to thirty-six hours in which she's able to conceive. Exhibit three: even if a baby is conceived, wild pandas will typically produce just one cub every two years—an exceptionally slow method of repopulating. (With twins, only one is cared for; the other one won't survive.) Exhibit four: there isn't enough good habitat left.

All of these criticisms have some merit. But they lose sight of an inconvenient fact: pandas were surviving on bamboo, were mating and conceiving and repopulating the species, and were roaming through plenty of good habitat for millions of years— before humans came along and changed the equation.

A panda at Wolong.

Critics also point to money. All that money that could help other species or other conservation efforts or tackle human problems such as homelessness or poverty—for one species?

But the panda (like the polar bear and the tiger, for example) has become a flagship species—a species people adore and flock to—and that popularity and visibility is something conservationists can, and do, build upon to broaden public awareness and support for a wider spectrum of conservation concerns.

"For some iconic species such as the giant panda, conservation successes can also help hundreds of lesser-known species that live alongside them," says Axel Moehrenschlager of IUCN. "By restoring species, associated habitat protection can have a huge, positive, collateral impact on all sorts of other creatures that would otherwise not get the attention.

"And I think that in those cases," he continues, "where you're able to demonstrate the return of a species that people care about—for whatever reason—it conveys a sense of hope at a time when many people feel helpless."

The panda bear has become the iconic flagship species for animal conservation in general. The tiger (Sumatran tiger shown here) is also a huge tourist attraction and draws attention to the trophy hunting and illegal poaching of wild animals. The polar bear has become the iconic symbol for the dangers of climate change.

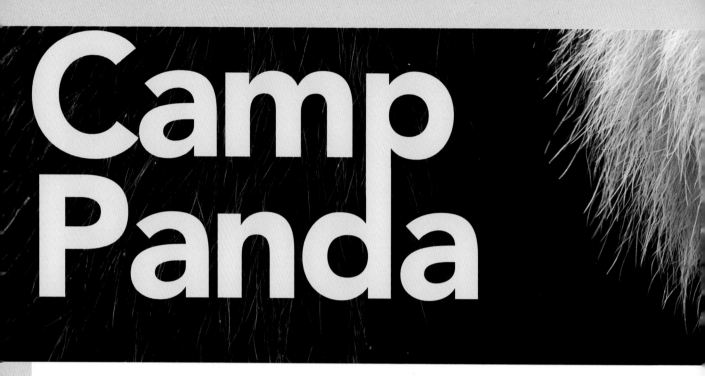

Camp Panda

Teeny-tiny panda cub Tao Tao—weighing in at approximately 4 ounces (about 1/900th the size of his mother)—was born in August of 2010, in a semi-wild training enclosure, delivered by his mama, Cao Cao, with no human intervention. After a three-year hiatus (spent restructuring the program and rebuilding after the earthquake), stage two of the panda reintroduction program began again in earnest. Tao Tao was the first captive cub born naturally, just as he would have been in the wild, showcasing right from the get-go a significant change in the three-stage training program.

Technically, stage one began before Tao Tao's birth. Team members placed a pregnant female panda in a semi-wild enclosure about one acre in size—with natural vegetation and a den where the soon-to-be mother could give birth. If the

Mama panda Cao Cao carries baby Tao Tao (about a month old here) in their enclosure. At this age, Tao Tao still can't walk and remains completely dependent on his mother. The discrepancy in size between a newborn panda and an adult panda (4 ounces at birth, growing up to 350 pounds) is the largest that exists among mammals.

cub was born healthy, both mother and cub would stay in the enclosure for about one year. Tao Tao was indeed healthy, and thus Huang Yan officially enrolled him in the training-to-be-wild camp right at birth, before he had any interaction with humans, before he had a chance to become accustomed to captive living.

Now, for the first time—as if it were Halloween or a day at a Disney theme park—Huang Yan's team don their panda suits whenever they enter the enclosure to clean it or deliver bamboo. But alas, they can't play with the huggable, lovable panda cub. Not even when he becomes truly irresistible as he learns to run a few steps (at about four months old) and roll around playfully.

The only additional interaction they'll have is for health checkups or, when the time comes, lugging the cub and his mama through tough mountain terrain to a new enclosure. They will, however, be monitoring the panda's behavior—twenty-four hours a day, seven days a week—using roughly one hundred video cameras placed throughout the enclosure that connect to a series of monitors in a small mission control–like room.

"Behaviorally, [the panda cubs] are assessed using a complex evaluation that looks at movement, climbing ability, communication, and interaction with the mother," explains Huang Yan of CCRCGP. "The behaviors we monitor include eating bamboo, locomotion, drinking, resting, sitting, exercise, investigating their surroundings, and scratching. The protocols are constantly being updated as the research progresses."

Only the healthiest and strongest cubs are candidates for release—they are the ones that graduate to stage two. It was clear that Tao Tao—in training with his mother—was acquiring skills much faster than the captive-bred cubs (as Xiang Xiang

Little Tao Tao having a medical exam—this time to check his weight. The scientist's panda suit is covered in panda pee and poo to mask his human scent. Pandas have a keen sense of smell—the strongest of their senses—and communicate with other pandas primarily through scent (even more than vocalizations). Each panda has its own scent—and that varies by gender and changes with age.

Measuring Tao Tao.

had once been). Tao Tao was a champion—so Huang Yan promoted him to the next training level, bringing him one step closer to freedom in the wild.

In this second stage, the enclosures cover about 300,000 square meters (or 74 acres), are higher in the mountains (thus colder), and have a much more diverse landscape than the prior enclosure. There are three such enclosures, which means three pairs of mothers and cubs train simultaneously (pandas are naturally solitary animals, which is why the enclosures are separated, one mother and her cub per enclosure). Here, with tougher terrain and with a much larger territory, Tao Tao faced greater challenges when it came to finding bamboo, water, and shelter. It was a more difficult and risky environment for him—slipping in mud on the mountainside, huddling in the cold, traveling longer distances through steep, rocky terrain to find food—but this was critical for training purposes, and critical for surviving in the wild. Plus, Mama had his back.

With humans out of the way, Mama Panda gave Tao Tao the paws-on training he'd need for survival. She taught him—by demonstrating—to seek shelter in caves or

Tao Tao climbs a tree in the training enclosure. His mama is right there for help and protection—nudging him a bit higher, ready to pull him down if he gets too high or isn't holding on properly.

hollow trees when the weather was icy cold. She taught him—by demonstrating—how to climb trees when he was just six months old, pulling him down by the scruff of his neck when he got stuck (lots of cubs get stuck!). She taught him—by demonstrating—how to pull up tasty bamboo stalks, strip them of leaves, and eat them.

Meanwhile, the team lingered in the background: the vet provided medical checkups and vaccinations when needed (checking for parasites, injuries, and disease; measuring weight and growth), and other team members monitored the pandas around the clock. They also staged tests—such as introducing Tao Tao to potential foes.

One day, Tao Tao was introduced to a "predator"—a clouded leopard stuffed toy, smeared with leopard pee and poo and plopped in the middle of the forest. Panda-suited scientists hid behind trees and watched as a curious Tao Tao ventured over to investigate. Suddenly, a leopard snarl and growl rang out through the trees (a recording played by the scientists). Tao Tao scurried away and scampered up a tree—the perfect response!

He was also introduced to such nonthreatening species as pheasants, pigs, and sheep and trained to recognize other pandas as his own kind. Tao Tao withstood rainstorms, frightening thunderclaps, and bone-chilling blizzards (luckily pandas have two coats of fur for warmth, and the undercoat is slightly oily for repelling water); he withstood mudslides that sent him slipping and sliding and tumbling down hillsides. The tests were many, but Tao Tao persisted in finding food and shelter and climbing trees all on his own.

In stage two, the goal is "basically to determine if they can survive in the wild on their own with no human intervention," explains Huang Yan. "Can they find water and bamboo? Can they survive the different seasons, as the amount of food can vary between seasons."

Assuming that the panda cub successfully meets the milestones of training, and that he remains healthy, he will be fitted with a radio collar for monitoring and moved to stage three—release into the wild habitat.

The radio signal emitted from the collar can be tracked. Thus the animals can be observed in the wild, their droppings analyzed for diet and health, and their habitat

Tao Tao up a tree on his own. Climbing trees is a must-have skill for survival—particularly if there is a predator, such as a leopard, around. Pandas don't have many natural predators—their greatest danger continues to come from humans.

inspected for particulars of daily living and survival—providing information on the size of their home territory, daily movements, periods of inactivity, and some behavioral data. The collars are designed to have a minimal effect on the pandas and thus on their behavior, and they don't seem to mind wearing them.

Mama Panda, having grown up in captivity, is too used to humans to be released. But at two years of age, cub Tao Tao was deemed ready for the wild—for going solo— just as nature intended.

In October of 2012, Zhang Hemin, Huang Yan, and their team released Tao Tao into the wild at the Lipingzi Nature Reserve. The site was chosen in part due to its low panda population—about twenty wild bears. The team hoped it would be easier here for Tao Tao to blend in and make his way with less competition for territory and food. Eight months after his release, Tao Tao had not been seen, but the radio-collar data indicated that he was healthy, had survived an unusually bitter-cold winter, and had had some interactions with other pandas—including, researchers think, mating.

Tao Tao is released into the wild wearing a radio collar. Once they're in the wild, the bears are elusive and often hard to spot, even with the collar. But, luckily, they poop a lot—up to forty times a day. This gives researchers something tangible to confirm a particular panda's whereabouts and movements. This is how pandas are counted in the wild—by collecting the panda poop in an area and analyzing DNA to confirm a specific individual.

Tao Tao was spotted in a tree one year after his release.

Then, a year after his release, a wave of excitement washed over the CCRCGP team. Using radio telemetry tracking, they spotted the elusive Tao Tao up in a tree, hiding—frightened of the humans approaching . . . a great sign! Using a tranquilizer gun, they dropped him from the tree into a net. Blood tests confirmed good health; he also had a weight gain of twenty-two pounds.

As the first panda bear released under the new protocols, Tao Tao seemed to be thriving—completely free, out in the wild.

Since Tao Tao's release, the reintroduction program continues to evolve. Zhang Hemin and Huang Yan continue adapting it as new research and evidence become available.

One new development? Going solo. Mama Panda is now removed from the second-stage enclosure a few months before her cub's release. By this time, the cub has already been wandering away from Mama for lengthy periods to feed and explore, so her absence isn't altogether jarring. Perhaps the cub sniffs and snuffles around looking for her, but it's unlikely that the cub is frightened. Going solo gives the cub the opportunity—and the challenge—of truly being on his own (again, pandas are naturally solitary), allowing for a more authentic experience of life in the wild and hopefully allowing for a smoother transition.

Adding to the fun is a new costume change. For this, team members will dress up as the humans they are—*taking off* their panda suits—in the last month or two before release whenever the cub has to undergo something unpleasant: such as getting a vaccination or being transported (usually not very comfortably) for longer distances. The team does this to reinforce that fear of humans—which, hopefully, has already been well established.

Also on the change docket is varying the season in which the cubs are released. Fall and winter releases will soon make way for spring or summer releases—in an effort to capitalize on the panda breeding season for a smooth transition.

"The 'panda-going-into-the-wild' project is at a very early stage," says Huang Yan, of CCRCGP. "We need to send the pandas back to nature at different times to work out the best time for release. Plus, we believe females will be more welcomed by wild pandas when they are in heat."

Camp Panda and the reintroduction program is slowly making progress—one release at a time—gathering information and learning more with each effort. By 2016, seven cubs had been released. But because it takes time to train the cubs, it will also take time to know whether the goal of reintroducing pandas to the wild will, in fact, be a success and will achieve a self-sustaining wild population.

Still, every ongoing attempt at saving the panda means two things: the species is not yet gone . . . and . . . there is still hope.

Two giant panda teddy bears wrap their arms around the roly-poly furball known as Tao Tao.

Hope Brings Success

One thousand eight hundred and sixty-four. That's how many pandas were, at last count, living in the wild. That number represents a sizable population increase—17 percent over the last panda count. It also represents a big win for pandas, and for conservation efforts worldwide.

And so, in September 2016, the IUCN removed the giant panda from its Red List of Threatened Species and reclassified it as Vulnerable. Decades of conservation efforts have begun to pay off.

Still, the IUCN cautions, *"It is critically important that these protection measures are continued and that emerging threats are addressed. . . . The giant panda will remain a conservation-dependent species for the foreseeable future."*

But to ensure it *has* a future in the wild, the thirty-three small, scattered panda populations must become self-sustaining—*not* dependent on humans and ongoing conservation efforts. It is why the panda reintroduction program has the power to

Tree-climbing lessons at Wolong. Adult pandas can, and do, climb trees, although it's mostly panda cubs who spend extended periods of time above the forest floor. Avoiding predators is critical—particularly when mama is busy eating bamboo all day and isn't nearby for protection.

make an enormous impact on saving the species. The more pandas in the wild, the greater the species' genetic diversity, the greater the chance that pandas will survive threats as they emerge. And more pandas will, hopefully, breed more pandas who will breed more pandas—increasing the chances for survival of the species through sheer numbers.

"One of the things that's really powerful about reintroductions is that they are incredibly hopeful," says Axel Moehrenschlager of IUCN, *"because they're not simply about slowing the bleeding of a conservation crisis; instead they're about restoring a species, ultimately restoring an ecosystem . . . it's correcting past wrongs and making things better."*

Past wrongs—due to human actions and inaction—are why pandas and so many other vulnerable and endangered species are now at risk of extinction. It is up to us, then, to help. Not only out of obligation, but as a recognition that our planet exists for all species (most of whom were here before us).

A recognition that the diverseness of species on Earth adds to the beauty, the wonder, the awe of the world around us.

A recognition that humans are also dependent on the complex ecosystems we have so carelessly put into peril: dependent for food, for water, for shelter—for our very survival.

A recognition that "Gone. Forever. Extinct . . ." doesn't have to happen on our watch.

"And if we can say, 'Hey, this species would have been gone, but conservation action saved it,' then this can compel the public to save many others," explains Axel. *"In this way, reintroductions have a broader, more powerful impact that will continue to grow in the future."*

ECOSYSTEM RIPPLE

Because of the interconnectedness of an ecosystem, when any species is thrown off balance, the whole system is weakened and a chain reaction of failures is set in motion. If the mountain gorilla or the elephant or the Galápagos penguin goes extinct, it will trigger a variety of unforeseen consequences—but one sure result is that a link in the natural food chain will be altered and countless other animals as well as plants in the ecosystem will be negatively affected. Ultimately, this ripple reaches people who depend on that environment for food, water, and resources.

Endangered animals (clockwise from top left): hawksbill sea turtle, African elephant, Amur leopard, Galápagos penguin, Puerto Rican crested toad, mountain gorilla.

Stepping Up to Save a Species— What Can You Do?

To help the giant panda, visit Pandas International at: www.pandasinternational.org.

Pandas International has many exciting and worthwhile ways to help with panda conservation, including the extremely popular program specifically for kids, Pennies 4 Pandas, where children can work together or alone collecting change to donate to panda conservation efforts. Kids get to share their fundraising stories and pictures on the website. There are even prizes to win!

Additionally, for the conservation of all species:

- Be informed. Learn how interesting and important various species are.

- Visit a National Wildlife Refuge, a National Park, or an accredited zoo (most of which are involved in massive conservation efforts).

- Refuse to purchase any products or souvenirs made from threatened or endangered animals, for example, ivory (raw or carved), some corals, tortoise shells (and products made from them, such as hair clips and bracelets), beluga caviar, tiger and rhino products (sold as good luck charms or medicinals), live monkeys or apes, and some crocodile and snakeskin products. Check that a product has a permit issued by CITES (Convention on International Trade in Endangered Species) to ensure that the item was not made illegally from an endangered animal.

- Adopt an animal of a species you love. The adoption is symbolic, but the adoption fee—generally around $50— goes directly to the conservation efforts for saving that animal. (Adoptions usually come with a small gift, such as a plush animal, a poster, an adoption certificate, or a tote bag.)

- Adopt a panda: www.pandasinternational.org.

- Adopt other endangered species: wwf.org.

Wolong panda Zhang Ka and her cub (top), and Xi Xi's cub (bottom).

- Protect habitat. Help your community protect wildlife areas in your neighborhood or close by.

- Make your home wildlife friendly: plant native plants; don't use herbicides and pesticides that pollute the soil and water and poison the animals.

- Recycle everything you can. Buy sustainable products whenever possible.

- Support conservation organizations by following their efforts through social media, signing petitions to lawmakers, and donating money if possible.

Glossary

acclimated: to become adapted to a new environmental situation.

adaptability: the capacity to fit into one's surroundings.

behavioral science: a branch of science that seeks to understand a species' actions and behaviors and use that knowledge to predict behavioral traits.

biodiversity: biological diversity within an environment as shown by the number of different species of plants and animals.

canopy coverage: the amount of shaded area below forest trees.

captive breeding: veterinarians assisting animals in captivity to breed and produce offspring.

captive management: when a team of scientists works on the health, well-being, and best breeding options and practices of animals in captivity.

conservationist: a person who is involved in the planned management of a natural resource or a species in order to prevent exploitation, destruction, or neglect.

DNA: a substance that carries genetic information in the cells of plants and animals.

ecological: of or relating to ecology.

ecology: a branch of science concerned with the interrelationship of organisms and their environments.

ecosystem: everything that exists in a particular environment: the living organisms (animals, plants, microorganisms) and the nonliving (air, water, soil), which are all interconnected and interacting.

encroachment: advancing beyond the usual or proper limits; moving beyond the boundaries and taking control of an area of habitat for one's own use.

endangered: at great risk of extinction because of reduction in population.

extinct: no longer living on our planet (also **extinct in the wild:** when none of a given species remains in the wild, but some are alive in captivity).

fragmentation (of habitat): divided into smaller pieces, as one large habitat is broken into smaller chunks and separated by such things as roads, dams, bridges, etc.

gene/genetics: a unit of heredity that is transferred from parent to offspring and determines some characteristics of the offspring; heredity and variation of organisms.

genetic diversity: the variety of characteristics in the genetic makeup of a species; genetic diversity serves as a way for species to adapt to changing environments.

habitat: the place or environment where a plant or animal naturally or normally lives and grows.

industrialization: the process by which an economy is transformed from one based primarily on agriculture to one based on manufacturing.

poaching: killing wild animals illegally.

propagation: the increase of an organism in population.

reforestation: planting trees and other plants in order to regrow and rebuild a forest that has suffered loss due to human or environmental causes (such as wildfires).

species: a category of biological classification made up of related organisms capable of interbreeding (breeding with one another to produce fertile offspring).

viable: capable of living.

vulnerable: at great risk; a step down in classification from "endangered" but still at risk of extinction if the population numbers do not continue rising.

Acknowledgments

The author wishes to thank the following people: Suzanne Braden, Pandas International; Axel Moehrenschlager, IUCN (International Union for Conservation of Nature) and Calgary Zoo; Huang Yan, CCRCGP (the China Conservation and Research Center for the Giant Panda); Colby Loucks, WWF (World Wildlife Fund); Caroline Hawkins, producer, *Pandas: The Journey Home*; Jianguo "Jack" Liu, MSU (Michigan State University); Sue Nichols, MSU; Andrea Muller, Pandas International; my fabulous editor, Ann Rider; editorial assistant, Lily Kessinger; and the remarkable team at Houghton Mifflin Harcourt.

Sources

Interviews with the Author:

Suzanne Braden; Huang Yan; Axel Moehrenschlager; Colby Loucks; Jianguo "Jack" Liu; and Caroline Hawkins.

Books/Publications:

"Conservation Science for Giant Pandas and Their Habitat." Presented at the 2009 International Congress for Conservation Biology, Beijing.

Gipps, J.H.W., ed. *Beyond Captive Breeding: Re-introducing Endangered Mammals to the Wild*. Oxford, UK: Zoological Society of London & Clarendon Press, 1991.

Goodall, Jane, with Thane Maynard and Gail Hudson. *Hope for Animals and Their World: How Endangered Species Are Being Rescued from the Brink*. New York City: Grand Central Publishing, Hachette Book Group, 2009.

Lindburg, D. G., and Baragona, K., eds. *Giant Pandas: Biology & Conservation*. Berkeley: University of California Press, 2004.

Liu, Jianguo, et al. *Pandas and People: Coupling Human and Natural Systems for Sustainability*. New York: Oxford University Press, 2016.

Lumpkin, Susan, and John Seidensticker. *Smithsonian Book of Giant Pandas*. Washington, DC: Smithsonian Institution Press, 2002.

Nicholls, Henry. *The Way of the Pandas: The Curious History of China's Political Animal*. New York: Pegasus Books, 2012.

Schaller, George B. *The Giant Pandas of Wolong*. Wildlife Conservation International and New York Zoological Society. Chicago: University of Chicago Press, 1985.

Soorae, P. S., ed. *Global Re-introduction Perspectives 2013: Further case studies from around the globe*. Gland, Switzerland: IUCN/SSC Re-introduction Specialist Group and Abu Dhabi, UAE: Environmental Agency–Abu Dhabi, 2013.

Zhi, Lu. *Giant Pandas in the Wild: Saving an Endangered Species*. New York: Aperture Books, 2002.

Films/Videos:

Hawkins, Caroline, producer. *Pandas: The Journey Home*. National Geographic Films, 2014.

Selected Digital Resources:

AZA (Association of Zoos & Aquariums). www.aza.org, www.aza.org/reintroduction-programs.

Center for Biological Diversity. www.biologicaldiversity.org.

China Conservation and Research Center for the Giant Panda. www.chinapanda.org.cn.

International Union for Conservation of Nature. www.iucn.org, www.iucnredlist.org, www.iucnsscrsg.org.

Michigan State University Center for Systems Integration and Sustainability. csis.msu.edu/content/pandas-and-people.

Molecular Biology and Evolution. Oxford Journals. mbe.oxfordjournals.org.

National Geographic. www.nationalgeographic.com.

Pandas International. www.pandasinternational.org.

San Diego Zoo. www.sandiegozooglobal.org.

Smithsonian's National Zoo & Conservation Biology Institute. nationalzoo.si.edu/animals.

State Forestry Administration of the People's Republic of China. www.forestry.gov.cn.

Wolong Panda Club. www.pandaclub.cn/english.

World Wildlife Fund. wwf.org.

CONSERVATION EXPERTS

Suzanne Braden is the cofounder of Pandas International, seen here wearing a partial panda suit on one of her many field visits. When she visited China after the devastating earthquake and saw firsthand the toll it took on the already precarious position of the endangered panda, Suzanne was moved to do everything in her power to help the plight of the pandas. Pandas International supports research, habitat protection and regrowth, provides radio tracking-collars, medical equipment, and public information and education in support of the panda centers managed by the CCRCGP.

Axel Moehrenschlager is seen here in the high mountain forests of Kenya where he is attempting to reintroduce the critically endangered mountain bongo antelope (of which only sixty remain in the wild). He became fascinated with reintroductions because he saw a way of interweaving innovation generated by science with direct conservation action to make an immediate, positive difference for species. Axel wants today's youth to understand there is hope for nature and that they, too, can make a difference. We will need their future leadership to build on the successes of today.

Huang Yan has devoted his adult life to panda conservation. He was part of the CCRCGP team that ultimately cracked the code and mastered captive breeding for pandas—a crucial first step in preserving and growing their numbers, and in diversifying the panda gene pool. Now, as deputy chief engineer and head of the reintroduction program for CCRCGP, his goal is to understand all aspects of the giant panda so that they can be released successfully into the wild and create a sustainable population.

Colby Loucks became involved in panda conservation through GIS—a software program that allows you to analyze and map things spatially. WWF China needed someone to look at satellite imagery and map the remaining panda habitat, and to make predictions on remaining pandas in the Qinling Mountains. Once he took on this project and was able to travel and see amazing landscapes, he was hooked on panda conservation.

Jianguo "Jack" Liu is the director and sustainability scholar at Michigan State University's Center for Systems Integration and Sustainability. He has spent more than two decades studying the pandas and people of Wolong, using a holistic approach that incorporates input from ecological, social, economic, and behavioral sciences. By combining the human and the natural systems approach, Jack has brought new solutions to panda conservation and conservation science in general.

Index